GOD SIGHTINGS

God Sightings

Discovering God
in Everyday Life

BASS M. MITCHELL

DIMENSIONS
FOR LIVING
NASHVILLE

GOD SIGHTINGS:
Discovering God in Everyday Life

Copyright © 2001 by Dimensions for Living

Library of Congress Cataloging-in-Publication Data

Mitchell, Bass M., 1955-
    God sightings : discovering God in everyday life / Bass M. Mitchell.

    p. cm.
    ISBN 0-687-09751-7 (alk. paper)
    1. Christian life—Meditations.   I. Title.
    BV4501.3 .M58 2001
    242—dc21

                                        2001032464

01 02 03 04 05 06 07 08 09 10—10 9 8 7 6 5 4 3 2 1

MANUFACTURED IN THE UNITED STATES OF AMERICA

Contents

Introduction

*W*HEN I WAS A TEENAGER, I WOULD GO TO SUM-
mer church camp at Cragmont near Black
Mountain in the majestic Great Smoky Mountains of North Carolina. To this very day when I
just say that name, "Cragmont," good feelings
and memories flood over me. For Cragmont was
a place where many of us had "mountaintop
experiences" like Moses on Mount Sinai and the
three disciples on the Mount of Transfiguration.

Mountaintop experiences are those times when
God is so real that you can almost see God,
almost touch God. They are the special, outside
your daily routine, encounters with the Creator of
the universe. Such encounters transform and
transfigure you. You take them with you down
the mountain to help you live in the valley.

Where is your Cragmont? Are there times or
places in your life that you look back on and say,
"There! God was there. God spoke to me. God
touched me, changed my life. I saw God. I heard
God."?

When Peter saw Jesus transfigured on the
mountaintop, Peter wanted to stay up there. He
wanted to hold on to his mountaintop experience.

Peter suggested that they build booths or shelters there for them all. He wanted to preserve that experience, to freeze it, to live on that mountaintop forever. Who can blame him?

In a way, that really isn't a bad idea. Mountaintop experiences are special. We need to preserve them. If there's a place where you have seen a vision of God or felt a unique sense of God's presence, build a shelter there and revisit it. If you can't literally go there, then go there in your mind and in your heart. Recall those times. In your own way, climb back up there and find renewal and strength for life in the valley.

Or maybe it's not a place at all for you. Maybe it's an activity, something you have done in the past through which you have really experienced the presence of God. A friend of mine tells me that music does this for him. It takes him right to the mountaintop. He told me recently, "Sometimes when I am singing certain hymns, God speaks so powerfully to me that I can't keep singing." He often goes back to those hymns and finds God once again through them.

I don't know where your mountaintop is or how you have experienced those special times with God. But I do know that it's good to revisit them. We can't live up there, however. After the Transfiguration, Jesus led Peter, James, and John down the mountain, back to the valley, to the real world; for that's where they had to live and work.

I confess to you that I have not had many mountaintop experiences. I have felt God's presence in many times and places; but times like Cragmont are rare, at least for me. After all, there was only one Transfiguration and only three of Jesus' disciples experienced it. Only Moses had those extraordinary sightings of God on the mountain.

My life has not been one primarily of leaping from one mountaintop to another. I would guess that it's been the same for you. The story of my life is that of daily sensing God's presence as I walk through the valleys. Every day I get glimpses, often in quiet, subtle, yet powerful ways, of God working in my life.

Remember Elijah? He was cowering in a cave from his enemies, listening intently for some sign of God's presence. First Kings 19:11-12 (KJV) reads,

> And [God] said [to Elijah], "Go forth, and stand upon the mount before the LORD. And, behold, the LORD passed by, and a great and strong wind rent the mountains, and brake in pieces the rocks before the LORD; but the LORD was not in the wind: and after the wind an earthquake; but the LORD was not in the earthquake: And after the earthquake a fire; but the LORD was not in the fire: and after the fire a still small voice.

I have more often seen and heard God in still, small, quiet ways and voices than in the spectacular mountaintop experiences. Sometimes I sight God when...I look out a window and see a mountain or a bird...I read or remember some word from the Bible just when I need it...a sense of unexplainable peace comes over me in a stressful situation...the thoughtfulness of a friend brings a kind deed or word my way...I am reminded of just how blessed I am. Quite often I see God in others—in their laughter, their compassion, their wisdom, and their friendship.

Surely you have experienced God in similar ways. Perhaps it was something you saw or read, or maybe it was while you were out for a walk. Perhaps you were simply looking out a window. Before you knew it, you caught a glimpse of God or you heard God speak to you in some still small voice, giving you an insight you needed or a reminder of something important you had forgotten or simply a reminder, "Hey. I'm still here. I will never leave you."

We cannot make the mountaintop experiences, those extraordinary encounters with God, the norm. We must not think that if we aren't having them all the time that something is wrong with our faith. Those mountaintop encounters are special gifts God gives us. We should cherish them. Revisit them. Draw strength from them. But we can't live there. God is as much, if not more so, in the valleys as on the mountaintops, if we will look and listen.

Some of my relatives were Cherokee Indians. I remember my grandfather telling us about "signs" and how to look for "signs"—tracks, sounds, movements that meant game were near. On walks through the mountains of the George Washington National Forest, I can't help but see the "signs" of all kinds of creatures, great and small. That's what I try to do each and every day, look for God sightings, for the "signs" that God is near.

This book, like my previous one, *In Every Blade of Rustling Grass,* is a collection of God sightings from my life. I offer them as examples of how you, too, might look and listen for "signs" of God each day of your life.

Exercise

Physical exercise has some value, but spiritual exercise is valuable in every way, because it promises life both for the present and for the future (1 Timothy 4:8, TEV).

SOME TIME AGO, MY DOCTOR SOUGHT TO CONVEY TO me the importance of keeping physically fit. "You must resist the temptation" (he used a religious word because he knows I'm a minister) "to hibernate," he told me. This was his way of telling me, "Arise, couch potato!" "Cut down on the salt," he continued, barking orders at me, reminding me of my baseball coach in high school. "And you must exercise thirty minutes at least four times a week. Got that?"

"Got it, coach," I mumbled.

He was mumbling something too as he picked up my chart and walked out. It was something like, "If it were not for the fact that the television and the refrigerator were in separate rooms, this guy would never get any exercise." I did not tell him that I was working on an invention combining the recliner with a refrigerator.

So, I decided to get more physical. At the time I was on the staff at First United Methodist Church in Charlottesville, Virginia, and was working with the youth. We kicked off our youth fall program at the home of one of the members of our church. Everything was going great until I walked by several of the boys playing basketball. They challenged me to join in. I thought that would not be too difficult and would make my doctor happy. Big mistake!

I can still see the images in my mind—young, muscular, Michael Jordan bodies soaring through the air to make lay-ups or jump shots over me, around me, through me, while I mostly panted for air.

And what a bunch of thoughtful kids. I mean, I cannot tell you how many times they walked by me and asked things like:

"Are you OK, Mr. Bass?"

"Need oxygen or anything?"

"Should we call the paramedics?"

Yeah, a great bunch of kids.

And I was the most popular player, if I say so myself. How thoughtful of them to make me feel so special, for they all wanted to guard me or have me guard them. Now you must admit that is downright considerate.

I tried a few moves from my youthful days spent on the court, only to miss every shot; travel; or get a large elbow across the nose, knocking my glasses across the court and my senses into the next state. Whoever said basketball was a "non-contact sport" probably never played, at least with these boys.

But the worst was yet to come. And it did—Monday morning. I woke up to discover every muscle I had, all two of them, felt like rubber bands twisted into knots. I was so stiff I could hardly get out of bed. My wife looked at me funny (but that is not unusual in the morning). My kids looked at me with a sad, embarrassed look that said, "Our poor dad. What a wimp." But I put on a happy face (my facial muscles also ached) and got to the medicine cabinet as quickly as possible. Thank God for aspirin!

I learned an important lesson that day: If you start using muscles that have not been used in a while, they let you know it really fast.

But guess what. It was not a bad kind of pain. In a way, it felt good to exercise, to use those muscles in ways I had not for a long time. Come to think of it, I am going to play basketball, soccer, baseball, football as often as possible......
NOT!!!

But I am going to exercise more. I need it. Soon the pain goes away. The muscles get used to it and grow stronger. The pain is replaced by strength, vitality, energy, and just a plain good feeling about yourself. Any doctor will tell you that moderate exercise is good for you.

You know, there are also some spiritual muscles many people have not used in a while, although it is just as important to get spiritual exercise as physical.

Use those spiritual muscles in your legs to get up and go to worship and church school on Sundays. Yes, it will be a little painful at first; but that is nothing in comparison to the benefits you will receive.

Flex those spiritual muscles in your back to reach down and take up some ministry in your church or community. Those muscles will get a little sore. I will not deny that. But that soreness will soon be replaced with an overwhelming sense of joy and fulfillment as you see others touched by God through you.

You can also use the spiritual muscles in your hands and arms to reach for your wallet or purse and to give the Lord tithes and offerings. This might be the most painful spiritual exercise possible. But it is essential for spiritual fitness. Giving reminds us that all we have comes from God and that we are dependent on God for all things. It says "Thanks!" for all God's blessings. But it also allows us the privilege of participating in the continuing work of Christ in the world.

What spiritual muscles most need exercising in your life right now? When you finish, how about a round of tennis? Surely I will be better at that than basketball.

Lord, I know I need to get more exercise, physical and spiritual. Help me not to be lazy or neglectful of either one. Help me to discover the blessings you give through them. Amen.

Children

Children are a gift from the LORD
(Psalm 127:3, TEV).

I SUPPOSE GOD HAS TAUGHT ME AS MUCH THROUGH children as through all the adult teachers I have had. Almost every Sunday, during children's time in the worship service, I learn something new from them. They have especially taught me the value of laughter. Usually that laughter has come at my expense, but I have gladly paid it. Sometimes, however, it comes at the expense of their parents.

I will never forget when our son, Michael, was about five. He went up front at children's time in another church. At the end, the pastor asked if anyone would lead them in prayer. Michael's hand went up while my wife, Debbie, and I began slipping down in the pew, since we never knew what Michael was going to do or say. Michael gave the only prayer he knew: "God is great. God is good. Let us thank God for our food. By God's hand we all are fed. Thank you Lord for our daily bread. Amen."

Then there was that Mother's Day when a nine-year-old boy named Jamie was in the group of children during children's time. I gave them each coupons from a little book concerning things they would give or promise their mother. One was to clean up their room. Another to take out the trash. One said, "A day without whining." I made the mistake of reading this and giving it to Jamie. Jamie promptly replied, "But my mother doesn't drink wine."

On another Sunday I told the children about all the wonderful animals God made. Then I let them name their favorite animals. One little boy named Jonathan said his favorites were fish. I made the mistake of asking him a question. (It's often risky business asking children questions. Because they *will* answer them!) "Jonathan, where do we find fish?" He promptly replied, "At Long John Silver's!" Everyone roared with laughter. And, most of us went to eat at Long John Silver's that day after the worship service.

At still another service I was telling the children a detailed story about when I was young and got lost in the woods. I told them about how dark and scary it was, especially as the sun set. "I heard an owl off in the distance," I said. And right then, little Jay, who was really into my story, looked up and asked, "Mr. Bass, did you ever find your way out?" When the laughter began to fade, I replied, "No, Jay, I never did."

Another time I told the children Jesus' parable of the lost sheep. Then I asked, "Why did the shepherd count his sheep each night as they went into the fold?" Caleb, about six years old, said, "So he could go to sleep." When some composure had been regained by the congregation and to tease him and his parents a little I asked, "Whose child are you, anyway?" Without blinking an eye, Caleb replied, "God's child." I did not ask him any more questions.

But I think my favorite was the little girl with blond curls hanging down on her shoulders. As she arrived at church one Sunday in the arms of her grandmother, she shouted loud enough for all to hear, *"Yea! God's house!"*

Lord, Isaiah wrote that "a little child shall lead them." They surely do. You teach us so much through them. Thank you for entrusting the children into our care. Help us to love and cherish them as you do. Help us to lead them to know and love you. Amen.

Stand Tall

Which of you by taking thought can add one cubit unto his stature? (Matthew 6:27, KJV).

O BVIOUSLY, JESUS HAD NOT BEEN TO A MALL AND was not a slave to fashions. Now we *can* add quite a few cubits to our height. I know. I have witnessed this phenomenon.

"Where?" you ask.

At my observational laboratory.

"Where is that?" you ask.

Why, it's the mall, of course.

If you are a sociologist or anthropologist or psychologist or "preachologist," then you hang out at the mall. You can learn much about the human creature there—what he desires, what she longs for.

Just recently I set up my observational blind near a shoe store. Teens of all shapes, sizes, hair colors, and assorted body rings were wandering in and out. I had picked a good spot.

Several young females were herded together outside the store, all of them looking down at the new shoes they had just purchased—at least I suppose they were shoes. They did give me some 70's flashbacks, for they were sandals with extremely thick soles—some several inches. It was clear that the girls absolutely loved these shoes, and the reason was also clear: The shoes made them taller and were fashionable, the "in thing" to own. I watched as they plodded down the mall, the sound of their platform sandals flopping on the tile, telling everyone that the girls were taller and also in style.

Later in the week I was home one day when my daughter, Meredith, came into the house. She hugged my neck (she still does that and I hope never stops). I immediately noticed something about her; she was taller and I said so. She beamed and said, "Oh, it's just my shoes." And sure enough, she had her own pair of skyscraper sandals. She was standing tall.

Teens, like most all of us, are seldom really satisfied with themselves. We aren't happy with our nose, or smile, or weight, or glasses. We're always looking for ways to improve ourselves, to make ourselves stand just a little taller. Nothing wrong with that I suppose—self-improvement, that is. A good, healthy instinct I would say, unless it goes too far.

The people on Madison Avenue sure have found a way to tap this need. Just think of all the products offered in countless television commercials aimed at making us taller, thinner, smarter, prettier, and _____er. You name the _____er and there's a product for it or will be soon. It is the American way, is it not—preying on insecurities or creating new ones, manufacturing new products that promise to give us more of the good life, things to make us better, taller than we are?

As I sat there in the mall that day, a rap song came over the **MUZAC**. And I found myself rapping out a song of my own:

Who wouldn't want to be a little taller?
and most of us could stand to be a little smaller.

Who wouldn't want to have brighter teeth,
more comfortable shoes for aching feet?

And what of Grecian Formula® for graying hair
or Rogaine® for hair that just ain't there?

Don't neglect your Calvin Klein®
to wear when you go out to dine.

And have you ordered your Wonder Bra®
or a year's admittance to the newest spa?

Order that video to improve your golf swing,
or take some lessons and learn to sing.

For your health, walk in the mall,
and make sure to use your Geritol®.

Improve your love life by visiting Niagara,
or better yet go buy some Viagra®.

Lose some weight with the newest diet,
it's easy as pie; go on and try it.

Buy some ginseng to make you smart,
use an aerobics video, good for your heart.

SURE® deodorant makes you feel fresh all day,
eat an apple to keep the doctor away.

Buy new shoes at your local mall,
and they'll make you stand really tall.

But maybe what we need isn't outside,
maybe we need to look deep inside.

For nothing outside can really make us tall
if inside we're feeling tiny and small.

But there's no answer looking inside us,
there's Someone else in whom we must trust.

If self-esteem is what we thirst,
Jesus said, "Put God first."

If this thing you can always do,
all else you need will be provided for you.

So if you want to stand real tall,
you don't have to go to the shopping mall.

*Lord, when I consider your love for me, it makes
me feel ten feet tall. Help me remember always how
much you love me and the whole world. Amen.*

Blessed Interruptions?

It is better to meet a mother bear robbed of her cubs than to meet some fool busy with a stupid project (Proverbs 17:12, TEV).

I KNOW WHAT YOU ARE THINKING, *BLESSED INTERRUPtions? You've got to be kidding! That's a contradiction in terms. Annoying, maybe. Bothersome, certainly. Obnoxious, troublesome, irritating, but not blessed. No way.*

We all know what it's like. We have our agenda, our "Things to Do List," and are busy doing them; and they just might be pressing things, things that really need our attention. Then, the phone rings. It's someone we know we'll be on the line with at least an hour, only an hour if we're lucky....

Or a neighbor drops by who has to tell us every detail of her latest operation....

Or the children call and want us to baby-sit, though we've just finished loading the car for a weekend trip....

That biblical writer who wrote the proverb on page 26 wasn't at all fond of interruptions. And let's confess, when we read these words, it is everything we can do to keep from saying, "AMEN!" For we all know that at least if we meet a mother bear robbed of her cubs, we have a chance of escaping. But there's no escape from the fool with a project.

I have come to see that maybe we shouldn't try to escape interruptions, however. In fact, they *can* be blessed. They can be opportunities God gives us to be a blessing to someone else or for God to give us a blessing. What matters is how we look at them. In fact, if we see interruptions as annoying, it's because we are the ones being interrupted. But if we are the ones doing the interrupting, if we need someone's time or attention, well, that's not an interruption, is it?

Jesus set the example for us, as in all things. He saw the potential for blessings in interruptions. Just read Mark 6 and notice how many interruptions Jesus had on a typical day and how he dealt with them.

Jesus had planned to take his disciples to a quiet place after they returned from a preaching and healing trip, for there were so many people around them that they did not even have time to eat. They got into a boat and headed up the coast of the Sea of Galilee. As they neared the shore, they heard a noise. They looked ahead; and there lined up along the shore were hundreds, possibly thousands of people. So much for getting away from it all.

How did Jesus respond to this interruption? The Scripture says that Jesus looked over the crowd and the image of hungry sheep came into his mind. They were sheep without a shepherd, hungry and lost, hungry for spiritual food. So, Jesus had compassion on them. He spent much of the day teaching them, providing for their spiritual nourishment, and then multiplying the loaves and fishes for their physical needs.

Later that night (Mark 6:53-56), Jesus and the disciples decided to go across the lake. Maybe they could get some peace and quiet over there. But when he got out of the boat, Jesus was immediately recognized.

Everywhere Jesus went, Mark tells us, needy people were brought to him. The Great Physician's waiting room was always crowded. How did he treat those who interrupted him? He tenderly ministered to each person brought to him.

Jesus' life was as busy and hectic as ours and more so. He had one interruption after another. But he lived by a simple rule. It was the Number One item on his agenda each day: Persons have priority. The needs of others took precedence over his own. There was always time for an interruption . . . for the woman with the issue of blood who reached out to touch the hem of his garment . . . for the unclean, despised leper. . . for the lonely blind man Bartimaeus . . . for a thirsty woman at a well who had failed in every meaningful relationship she ever had . . . for a good-for-nothing thief on the cross beside him who asked to be remembered. Imagine that. His life's blood was draining from his body and Jesus had time for an interruption, for someone in need. He always has time for us, too. Whenever we need him, whatever the situation, he's never too busy. I think that's how he would like us to be for one another.

Do you have call waiting on your telephone? It's a service you can get from the phone company. You're talking on the phone and suddenly you hear a little beep. The beep tells you someone else is trying to call you. So, you press a button, put the person you're talking with on hold, and answer the other call.

Perhaps we need a kind of spiritual call waiting in our lives. We are surrounded by people who need us, who need our attention; but often we are so wrapped up in our own lives and conversations that they go unnoticed. I have promised myself that I will try to be more sensitive and alert for those little "beeps," those interruptions that so often fill my days, not seeing them as interruptions but as opportunities to be a blessing and to receive one. Will you join me?

Lord, it's me again. Hope I'm not interrupting. Amen.

Listen

You must understand this, my beloved: let everyone be quick to listen (James 1:19).

ONE OF THE GREATEST BLESSINGS WE CAN BESTOW on someone else is the gift of listening. We should get some hint about the importance of listening from how the Creator has made us—with two ears and only one mouth.

One of the things that attracted people to Jesus was that he was a good listener. He gave them his undivided attention. He really listened and understood what they were saying and what they needed.

I have found that listening begins at home. When a family member interrupts me with an obvious need or concern, I should give him or her my undivided attention. But you know what? I have discovered to my dismay that I am more understanding and patient with others sometimes than I am with my family.

Pastors can be the world's worst listeners. I read once about a pastor who every Sunday asked persons to write on and turn in a card if they needed a pastoral visit. One Sunday after the service he was shocked when he received several cards—one from his wife and one from each of his children.

I was taking my daughter, Meredith, to gym class one day in Charlottesville, Virginia, and was deep in thought about something. She was busy telling me everything that happened to her that day. Suddenly, she grew quiet. I looked at her and she said, "Daddy, are you really listening or just pretending?"

We need to listen to our children. Did you hear about the family who had the pastor over for an evening meal? Throughout the meal the little boy tried unsuccessfully to get his father's attention. His father kept telling him, "Later. The adults are talking right now." Finally, the father said, "Okay, son. What is it that you just can't wait to say?" The little boy said, "There was a grasshopper in the salad. But it's OK now. The minister just ate it." It pays to listen.

Others are also needing desperately for some-one to care enough to listen. Once I was on a plane to California where I was to conduct some church school teacher training workshops. A man was sitting beside me whom I had never seen before. I was busy trying to look over my notes and plans. Before long, this man was telling me his life's story, to my dismay. He was going through a bitter divorce and child custody battle.

He was shaking with emotion and tears filled his eyes. I felt ashamed of myself for feeling anger at being interrupted. After he had poured out his heart to me, he asked what I did. I told him I was a minister. Right there in the plane he asked me to have a prayer with him and for his family. Afterward, he told me how much better he felt. I had done nothing but listen. But listening is a great gift.

Reverend Gregory was a retired United Methodist minister who lived in Alleghany County, Virginia. A few years ago his wife died. And not long after that he lost two sons. He was telling me what a tough time that was, especially the days and weeks after the funerals. But then he told me about a dear lady who dropped by one day, sat down in his house, and simply said, "I'm here to listen." And he poured out his heart to her.

"I'm here to listen." Not a bad slogan for Christians, is it?

Lord, I thank you that you always listen. You always care. Help me listen with both ears and with all my heart to those who just need someone to take a little time to hear them, to care for them. Amen.

The
John the Baptist
Test

You should think of us as Christ's servants
(1 Corinthians 4:1, TEV).

W HEN I WAS A YOUNG MINISTER, AN ELDERLY
minister took me aside one day and gave me the
best advice I think I have heard in regard to being
a leader in the church. He called it, the "John the
Baptist Test."

I interrupted him, respectfully. "You know, I'm
in seminary and I've had about all the tests I want
for a while."

"True," he noted, "but this is the most important test of all. This test determines whether you
truly pass or fail. And you take it every day in
countless ways."

"Wonderful," I replied, not so respectfully this
time. "Just what I need."

Ignoring me, he continued. "You know John
the Baptist, of course?" he asked.

I gave him that all-knowing-I've-gone-to semi-nary-look.

"Well, anyway," he continued, "John the Baptist had only one goal uppermost in his mind. Know what it was?"

I hated to admit it, but I did not remember that one from seminary.

"It's simply this," he said. "Of Jesus, John said, 'He must increase, but I must decrease.' That's John 3:30, in case you are wondering."

I was not wondering about the reference but just what it meant. I was beginning to think maybe this elderly minister had been preaching just a bit too long.

"That's the 'John the Baptist Test' all of us leaders must take and pass," he said. "To not care about any personal praise or criticism too much but to do all we can to decrease ourselves in order to magnify Christ. We are just signposts pointing not to ourselves but to him. That's the test that really matters."

I left him that day wishing he had been one of my professors in seminary... or maybe he was.

In 1 Corinthians 4, Paul writes about leaders and the important role they play in the church. In his own way, Paul presents the "John the Baptist Test" to all who would be leaders in the church. He says that leaders are just servants of Christ, stewards who have been honored with tasks, but who, in the end, are still just servants. Their highest concern is that Christ might increase and they decrease, so that the church might also grow and magnify Christ in its life and work.

Loving God, give us leaders who see themselves as servants, not ones to be served. Help us lift them up constantly in our prayers. Could it be, Lord, that you are also calling me to be a servant-leader? Do I pass or fail the "John the Baptist Test"? Amen.

Claiming Our Gifts

Now there are varieties of gifts, but the same Spirit; and there are varieties of services, but the same Lord; and there are varieties of activities, but it is the same God who activates all of them in everyone. To each is given the manifestation of the Spirit for the common good (1 Corinthians 12:4-7).

Whatever gift each of you may have received, use it in service to one another, like good stewards dispensing the grace of God in its varied forms.... In all things so act that the glory may be God's through Jesus Christ (1 Peter 4:10-11, NEB).

THEY LOOKED KIND OF SAD JUST LYING THERE IN THE corner of the room. There were about ten of them. They were decorated in brightly colored paper with large bows and frilly ribbons. Each one had someone's name on it. They were presents, gifts left over from a church Christmas party many months before—still wrapped, just lying there unclaimed, unused.

Each time I passed them I wondered what they contained. Some fabulous gifts could be hidden beneath that wrapping paper. Maybe there were gifts that would brighten someone's life. Maybe there were gifts someone really needed. But the persons would never know because they failed to claim the gifts. What a waste.

In 1 Corinthians 12, Paul talks about spiritual gifts. He says that the same Spirit gives gifts and that each person is given gifts. These are gifts (abilities, talents) to be used for the "common good." In other words, these gifts empower us for service in the church and world.

Christmas gifts are not the only ones that can remain wrapped and unclaimed. Too often spiritual gifts can be left lying in the corners of our lives. They are wondrous gifts. They could really make a difference in the world. They could be unwrapped and used to enrich the ministry of the church.

I am constantly amazed how gifted every Christian is. Almost daily I discover some gifts in persons that I was unaware of, and maybe they were too. That is very much the task I see for myself and all pastors. Our job is not to do ministry in place of the laity but to help them discover and use their gifts for ministry. We are gift scouts, like talent scouts, always on the lookout for God's gifted people.

The mission of the church is an immense one. It is too great for any one person or even a dozen. The gifts of every member of the church family are needed. Can you imagine what would happen in the life of your church if all your members claimed and unwrapped all their gifts?

Each of us, from the oldest to the youngest, has gifts for ministry. Some, we have claimed and use. Others, like unclaimed Christmas presents, still lie unclaimed in the corners of our lives. I challenge you, and myself, to pick up our gifts, to claim them, to unwrap and use them. The unusual thing about the gifts God gives is that the only way to truly receive them is to give them away.

Giver of all good gifts, how wonderful you are. You call us to service and give us all the gifts we need to serve. Thank you for all the gifts you give. Help us to unwrap and use them for the "common good," so that you may be honored and glorified. Amen.

Let Me Lend a Hand

Bear ye one another's burdens, and so fulfill the law of Christ (Galatians 6:2, KJV).

I STOOD ON MY FRONT PORCH AND WATCHED A NEIGHbor struggling to carry a heavy box into his house. So I called out, "Can I lend a hand?"

"No, thanks," he called back. "I can handle it myself."

As I turned to go inside, I heard a loud crash. My neighbor had dropped the box. It had a new television in it. I quickly went inside to spare him any further embarrassment.

Why didn't he let me help him?

One lovely fall morning a close friend went into his basement and took his own life. He was, evidently, carrying something extremely heavy. He didn't have to carry it alone.

Why didn't he let me help him?

Paul makes a point in Galatians 6:2 that is often unnoticed. We cannot bear one another's burdens unless we are willing to share our burdens. Have you ever wanted to help someone carry something heavy or deal with a problem, but he or she wouldn't let you? Turn that around. How many persons have wanted to help you deal with something heavy, and you refused to share that burden with them?

It is easier sometimes to help bear the burdens of others than to share our own burdens with others. When we help bear others' burdens, we are operating from a position of strength. That feels good. It boosts our ego. However, the sharing of a burden requires a different attitude and feeling. It is, in a way, a confession of weakness. It shows that we are not always adequate. To share a burden can be a humbling experience.

It seems that men find burden-sharing especially difficult. We hear a message early in our lives that real men are self-sufficient, independent, don't take charity from anyone. Big boys just don't cry. Ever.

A man I knew had been under great stress in his job. Finally, one night, be broke down and sobbed in his wife's arms for an hour. He actually believed that she could not love him after that, after he had been so weak. The truth was, as she told him, she loved him even more. He had been shutting her out; and now he had let her into his soul, his heart. They were closer than ever. She could not resolve his problem, but just telling her about it greatly lessened the load he was carrying.

It's selfish to hoard our burdens. It shuts out those who love us. It says, "I don't need you or anyone. I can make it by myself." But sharing a burden says the opposite: "I need you. I can't make it alone. I trust you. Please help me."

Who doesn't need to say those words from time to time?

Who doesn't need to hear them?

Lord, help us to be willing to bear the burdens of others and to share our burdens with others. Amen.

Brother Love

If any want to become my followers, let them deny themselves and take up their cross and follow me (Mark 8:34).

WHEN I WAS AT MOUNT OLIVE COLLEGE, IN Mount Olive, North Carolina, during the early seventies, the thing to wear, as a Christian, was a three-piece leisure suit and the biggest cross necklace one could find. We still have one picture of me with my cross. Whenever my wife, Debbie, needs a good laugh, she takes that picture out and looks at it.

I suppose we thought we were really taking up the cross. But I think Jesus had something very different in mind. He asked his disciples to be so totally committed to him that they would willingly take up crosses for his sake. Crosses are difficult, costly duties we choose to take on that we could avoid. They are responsibilities and ministries that we know will cost us a lot—our time, our energy, our money, and maybe even our lives— but we take them up anyway because we love Christ.

Taking up crosses is a personal choice. Crosses are not things we *have* to bear; they are tasks and burdens we *choose* to bear for Christ's sake. Jesus said, "...take up their cross...." That's a conscious, free decision. It's something we willingly accept, not some situation or inconvenience we cannot do anything about.

When I went to East Orange, New Jersey, years ago, I met a man they called "Brother Love." His name was Frank Love. A good name for him. In East Orange, as in most large cities, there are many homeless, hungry people. This man saw this great cross lying in his city and placed it on his back. He started a mission in downtown East Orange. Every day he is there feeding the hungry, finding the homeless places to sleep, helping the unemployed get jobs, calling the parents of the runaways he takes in, and witnessing to them all. In a few short years this mission has ministered to thousands of persons.

Brother Love teaches and preaches to these people throughout the week. Then he takes them to his church for Sunday school and worship services. I'll never forget standing before the group from his mission that Sunday morning. There must have been about twenty-five people with him. Most were poorly dressed. But they were there. And they knew their Sunday school lesson.

I found out from others later about all the sacrifices Brother Love has made. He gives his time and a lot of his money. He cooks. He cleans up. He's called at all hours of the day and night. He goes to the jail and takes custody of people. The burdens and problems of these needy persons are always on him. In many ways that cross has been heavy for him. It's taken much out of him. But you would not know this from talking with him.

I don't know if I've ever met a Christian more full of joy than Brother Love. He'll be the first to tell you he'd do it all over again. The sacrifices don't bother him. He told me, "It's been worth it all. I've seen persons others have given up on come to accept Christ and become new persons. I've seen their lives changed. And I've heard the relief and thanks of parents as I've called them and told them that their runaway children were with Christians who cared for them."

No one made Brother Love do this. It wasn't forced on him. It was a cross no one else saw or cared to see. He saw it! And he took it up!

I remember a man in a church I pastored. This man worked hard every day. But do you know what he did when he got home? He went over to a neighbor's house, an elderly man who could not care for himself. Every day he took this man his supper. Every day he bathed and shaved this man. He could have ignored the situation. He could have rightly said, "I'm too tired when I get home." He could have used those hours after work to go fishing, or play golf, or any number of things. Instead, he chose to use that time to take up a cross for Christ.

Lord, show me the cross you would have me take up for you each day. No matter what it costs me, it can never repay all you have done for me. Amen.

Cups of Water

For whosoever shall give you a cup of water to drink in my name, because ye belong to Christ, verily I say unto you, he shall not lose his reward (Mark 9:41, KJV).

A GROUP OF MEN FROM OUR CHURCH WAS HELPING a member of the church named Kyle who had recently suffered a heart attack. He was unable to fulfill his duties as a caretaker for a large estate. The leaves needed to be raked, so one Saturday we gathered at the estate and went to work. It was a hot day in October. Raking the leaves stirred up clouds of dust, and soon we were covered with it. We could taste it. Dorothy, Kyle's wife, came out with a large tray of glasses and pitchers of ice cold spring water. It was a kind and thoughtful thing she did, and it was the best glass of water I have ever had. We all said, "Thank you," many times.

She replied, with tears in her eyes, "No, thank you. We were thirsty and you have given us many glasses of water."

Some of my friends looked a little puzzled. Not

one recalled ever giving her or her husband any water. Then I told them what Jesus said about giving a cup of water. They began to smile as they finished their glasses of water and went back to raking leaves.

Little cups of water, small things we do for others out of love for Christ and for neighbor, may seem small indeed. But a cup of water offered to someone who is thirsty means more than perhaps we can know.

One of the joys of my life was teaching an Old Testament course in the Seymour Johnson Air Force Base Educational Center in Goldsboro, North Carolina. I got to know many of those men and women well. I found a growing love and respect for them.

One young man in the class had some serious medical problems. A couple of years before he had been assigned to help tear out the ceiling in a building. He did not know that it was made of asbestos. The falling asbestos particles got into his ear. Now this was causing him all kinds of problems. He had some tests run to determine if the asbestos had caused cancer. He underwent surgery on his ear.

Perhaps you can imagine what he and his wife must have been feeling all this time. They had no family on base and very few friends. He had to miss class frequently. So during this time I kept calling him to see how he was doing and to give him the assignments. I told him that I was praying for him. He came through the surgery, and so far there has been no trace of cancer.

The last day of class this young man and his wife came up to me with tears in their eyes, took hold of my hand, and told me how much my calls had meant to them. I could tell that they were really touched. I remember feeling a little surprised. I had forgotten, you see, how much a little cup of water could mean to those who are thirsty.

They do not seem like much, Lord, these little cups of water. But help us to carry a supply of them wherever we go, for we know they mean much to the thirsty souls you will bring across our path. Thank you, too, for the ones you have given us who had pitchers of water for us just when we needed them. Amen.

Water

Do you not know that all of us who have been baptized into Christ Jesus were baptized into his death? Therefore we have been buried with him by baptism into death, so that, just as Christ was raised from the dead by the glory of the Father, so we too might walk in newness of life (Romans 6:3-5).

WATER...

I remember standing with my brother on the banks of the Neuse River in Bridgeton, North Carolina while we watched a minister in hip boots wade out into the water. A line of people dressed in white robes stretched along the shore. Each one took a turn being dunked in that river. My brother observed, "You know, someone could get killed doin' that."

Only later after my own baptism and years of reflection have I come to understand that this is exactly the purpose of baptism. It is a grave in which we are buried, only to rise to a new life.

Water...

I joined a Boy Scout troop with a cabin on a riverbank where we held our meetings. I still remember those strong young lads picking me up and carrying me to the river, as they did every new scout, and shouting as they swung me back and forth, "One, two, three..." and sending me soaring through the air and into the river. I didn't mind it (for throwing a bass in the river is about like throwing Br'er Rabbit into the briar patch). I was laughing with everyone else, for I knew it meant I really was now a part of the troop. I was one of them.

When we enter the waters of baptism, we, too, are initiated into a troop, a family—God's family. Baptism means we have been adopted as sons and daughters of God. We are accepted. We belong to Christ, to his church, to each generation of Christians throughout history. We belong. We always will.

Water...

When we visited Niagara Falls one summer, I sat in amazement and watched the waters flowing through the power plant that tapped just a little of the awesome power the falls produce. The water turns great turbines that generate electricity.

The waters of baptism are also powerful and empowering waters. Jesus is baptized; and immediately the Holy Spirit descends upon him, empowering him for the work he is then just beginning. Likewise, baptism means the Holy Spirit flows in us like a mighty river, stirring turbines and generating energy so that we can live this new life we have been given in Christ and can continue his work.

Giving Lord, we use water each day, water that is one of your good gifts to us. Each time we use it, let it remind us of the new life you give in Christ; that we belong to you and your family; and that you flow through us, empowering us to do your work in the world. Amen.

Voices and Choices

*Then Jesus was led up by the Spirit
into the wilderness to be tempted by
the devil (Matthew 4:1).*

I CONFESS TO LOVING CARTOONS. MY FAVORITES ARE Disney cartoons with Goofy, a dog who's always getting into trouble of some kind. In one of them, Goofy is being tempted to do something he knows he should not do. He has a little angel on his left shoulder and a little devil on the other shoulder. Both are whispering in his ear, giving him contrary advice. Goofy listens to the little devil, who promptly flies over to the little angel and knocks him off his perch.

Doesn't it seem like there's often a little angel and a little devil on our shoulders? So many voices, so many choices...each and every day in so many different ways.

I started a diet this week, or tried to. I did so great Monday, just eating a salad and a few veggies at the K & W in Roanoke, Virginia. But on the way home, that little devil spoke to me constantly, "Hey, there's a Burger King up ahead. Wouldn't a Whopper Jr. taste good about right now?" But another voice said, "No, you don't want to do that. You've done so well today. You feel better already." The closer I got to it, the louder the first voice became, "There it is! Just a few more yards ahead. Turn in. Go ahead. You don't even have to get out of the car. There's the drive thru." "Don't do it," the second voice said; but weaker this time. Well, like Goofy, the angel got knocked off my shoulder.

A friend of mine told me how one day she was in the mall and saw this lovely dress in a store window. It was a budget buster, but a little voice kept telling her that there was no harm in trying it on. So she did. As she stood in front of the mirror, the voice told her how good it made her look and reminded her that she still had some room before she "maxed out" her credit card. When she whispered out loud, "Get thee behind me, Satan," the voice promptly came back, "My, girl, it looks just as good from back here."

Voices and choices...we really can't avoid them. Which we listen to makes all the difference in who we are, how we live.

A voice tells us to be faithful and committed to our spouse. But another voice may make us wonder if maybe someone else might be more interesting or better for us.

Voices and choices...we human beings have

always had them, even at the beginning. Eve is walking through the garden and sees the forbidden fruit. She hears God's voice, "Don't eat of that tree or you will surely die. Trust me. I know what's best for you." But another voice comes to her, "Did God really say that? Just look at that fruit. Doesn't it look delicious?" Then the first voice comes back to her, "Don't eat that fruit. You will die." "You won't die," the second voice says. "You'll just be smarter, and God doesn't want that. Why, you'll become a god. So go ahead."

Voices and choices. Adam and Eve did not listen to God's voice but to the wrong voice and made the wrong choice...as so often do we. But there came one, a human being like you and me, Jesus, by name, to the Jordan long ago. There he was baptized and heard the tremendous affirmation, "You are my beloved Son, and with you I am well pleased." Immediately he found himself in the wilderness...and the voices and choices came. "Since you are the Son of God, be God-like. You're hungry. Use your power to feed yourself and those hungry people. They'll love you for it, and you'll get a following. Why, just a thought from you and those round stones there, don't they look like loaves of bread, can become bread." But another voice echoed in the ears of Jesus and came forth from his mouth, "Human beings cannot live by bread alone." In other words, I will trust in God to provide for me.

The first voice persisted: "Everyone knows that the Messiah is to appear on the pinnacle of the Temple and then to leap down without being hurt. You could easily do that. Why take the long route? Take a shortcut. No need walking here and there, just dazzle them with your power. Angels will not let you get hurt. And what an impression you'll make." The voice even quoted Scripture this time. But God's voice came again into the heart and mouth of Jesus, "The Scripture also says, 'Do not put the Lord your God to the test.'"

Still the first voice came back: "Why not be whatever they want you to be? They don't want someone who identifies with sinners like you just did in the river. They want political power and freedom. They want a warrior to overthrow the Romans. I can give you that power and authority. Think of the good you can do as their king. Just bow down to me and it's done." But the other voice came, "Go away, Satan! The Scripture says, 'Worship the Lord your God and serve only him.'"

Voices and choices . . . even for Jesus, but Jesus knew which voice to say "Yes" to and which to say "No" to. Jesus kept saying "Yes" to God by becoming a servant, by giving his life.

I have always loved reading Greek mythology. Remember the one about Odysseus and the Sirens? The Sirens were monsters who lived on an island. Day and night they would send the sound of their sweet and enticing voices over the sea, seeking to lure sailors and ships to their island, where they would crash into the shore and die. Odysseus escaped them by blocking his crewmen's ears with bee's wax and tying himself to the mast, telling his men not to obey any of his orders when passing by the Isle of Sirens. He was the only man ever to hear their song and live. Later, Jason and the Argonauts were saved from the Sirens by the musician Orpheus, who drowned out the Siren singing with the music from his harp and his own wondrous voice.

The voices of evil that make us want to go our own way rather than God's way, to live just for ourselves, to do things that are not good for us, are powerful voices. The only way we can resist them is by lashing ourselves to Christ; following him into the wilderness; taking on a spiritual discipline like prayer, Bible reading, or fasting that will sharpen our listening skills. This will so fill our ears with God's voice, with God's music, that the other voice is drowned out . . . and we are left empowered, like the sons and daughters of God we are, to make and carry out the right choices, to be God's servants like Jesus.

Lord, when we do not know what to do or what to believe, help us to listen for your voice and to follow your guidance. Amen.

Scary Bridges

The angel of the LORD encampeth round about them that fear him, and delivereth them (Psalm 34:7, KJV).

God will put his angels in charge of you / to protect you wherever you go (Psalm 91:11, TEV).

Never despise one of these little ones; I tell you, they have their guardian angels in heaven, who look continually on the face of my heavenly Father (Matthew 18:10, NEB).

What are the angels, then? They are spirits who serve God and are sent by him to help those who are to receive salvation (Hebrews 1:14, TEV).

I GUESS MY FASCINATION WITH ANGELS BEGAN WHEN I was about ten years old. I had graduated to the Intermediate Sunday School Class in my home church. I remember lots of good things about that class, especially Mrs. Lib, the teacher. She was a kind, elderly lady who insisted that we memorize a different Bible verse each Sunday, something I was not grateful for at the time but give thanks for now.

There was a painting on the wall in our classroom that I stared at and wondered about for a long time. It was a painting of two children, a boy and girl, stepping across a wooden bridge that spanned a river far below. The water churned and swirled like a hungry beast ready to swallow the children. Jagged dark rocks, like teeth, rose from the water. The ropes and boards of the bridge were old and rotten. Some boards were cracked and missing. Yet the children did not seem to be aware of the danger all around them. My first thought was, *Is this really the kind of picture you want to hang around us kids? I mean, I have enough things to worry about without having to look at those two kids up there every Sunday and wonder if they made it.*

Then one Sunday I noticed something in the picture I had not seen before. In the watery mist behind the children, the artist had painted the beautiful face of an angel, their guardian angel, Mrs. Lib later explained to us. The angel was watching over the children, with strong arms stretched out toward them. The picture was making a striking contrast between the danger and the protecting presence of God's angel.

Angels. What a beautiful, comforting way to

describe God's loving care and protection. Wherever we go, God watches over us.

In a way, living can be like crossing the shaky bridge in that painting. Dangers loom around us. Some of them we see; but, like those children, sometimes we do not see the dangers. We walk out on a rickety old bridge and don't even know it.

I remember visiting a couple whose son was just learning how to walk. There was something unusual about their whole house, but I couldn't quite figure out what. Then I realized that every sharp table corner, anything that this little child could fall on while he was stumbling everywhere, had been removed or had padding placed over it. The child stumbled around, not realizing that his parents were protecting him. I wonder how often God pads the sharp corners or moves aside the dangers in our paths—and we are not aware of it.

On Easter Sunday, Michael, my six-year-old son, was behind me as we rode a dirt bike around my father-in-law's farm. We were having a great time going up and down the old dirt trails. But we (I should say "I") had foolishly forgotten to put on our helmets. You see, we were stepping onto a rickety, rotten bridge and didn't even know it. Suddenly, the back wheel locked up, throwing us off. Michael fell to the side, and I went over the handlebars. Michael was breathing, but I could not get him awake. Dazed and numb, I carried his limp body back to the house, terrorized each step with the thought that I had killed my son.

Well, by the time I got back to the house, Michael had regained consciousness. We went to the emergency room and had x-rays taken. Michael didn't have a scratch on him. He was fine. My face was badly scratched, and my thumb was broken.

For some time after that a cold shiver ran up my spine whenever I thought about our experience or even saw a motorcycle. For I realized that we both easily could have been killed.

Now those feelings have been replaced with ones of praise and thanksgiving. I know in my heart that God must have been with us, that our guardian angels were alert that day.

Still, when we go back to the farm for a visit, Michael asks me with a grin, "Dad, want to take a ride?" Then he holds out two helmets.

Whenever my wife and children go on a trip or every day when they leave for work and school, I have a fear for their safety in the back of my mind. But it's not nearly as great as it once was, for I find myself naturally entrusting them into God's loving care. I'm at peace about it. For I don't just see the dangerous old bridges they might cross, I look just a little higher for the faces of angels God has watching over them.

God of love, how you surround us with your loving care, even sending angels to watch over us.

What comfort this gives us, Lord; for we, your children, often find we have walked onto a scary bridge. Give us vision, Lord, that we might see the bridges before we step out onto them. But when we do not, give us the faith that helps us look up until we see the faces of your angels. Amen.

The Bird Watcher

Are not five sparrows sold for two pennies?
Yet not one of them is forgotten in God's
sight. But even the hairs of your head are all
counted. Do not be afraid; you are of more
value than many sparrows (Luke 12:6-7).

ONCE WE LIVED IN A FARMHOUSE JUST OUTSIDE Goldsboro, North Carolina. We had a large yard covered with beautiful green grass. Fruit trees of every kind decorated the yard, filling the spring with the sweet fragrance of their blooms and the summer and fall with their delicious fruit. No wonder all kinds of birds could be found in our yard most any time of the day.

"I bet they go and tell their friends about our yard," my son observed.

Maybe they did. Some would fly away; and soon more would come, coasting in for a landing like small airplanes or diving skillfully through the tree limbs to settle on just the right branch.

Our family would spend whole afternoons watching the birds. We would get out the encyclopedia and try to identify each species. We sat in amazement at the diversity and in envy as they seemed to lift themselves so easily into the air, soaring high and low.

"You might say that we are bird watchers," my wife commented one day.

"Jesus said that God is a bird watcher too!" I replied and quoted Luke 12:6.

Sparrows were very common birds in the time of Jesus. They were used for food by the poor and were sold quite cheaply—less than one-half a cent each. If you spent two cents, you could get a bargain—four sparrows and an extra sparrow thrown in. That's how little value sparrows had.

Jesus used this illustration from everyday life to help us understand what God is like. Even the little extra forgotten sparrow that's thrown into the deal is precious to God. If God cares so much for that sparrow, then just try to imagine how much God cares for each of us.

Many people feel or are made to feel that they are as worthless as one of those little sparrows. They don't matter. They're nobodies. Maybe you feel like that sometimes. But Jesus wants us to know we do matter. We are not faceless, nameless beings in a vast universe. Jesus tells us that God knows and cares for us as individuals. We are not nobodies. We are somebodies. Every person is of infinite value and worth to God.

When I explained all this to my family that day, my son observed, "So what Jesus was saying was that God is a bird watcher and a people watcher. Is that right?"

"That's exactly right," I replied, a little surprised at his insight. I told him, "Next time you can do the explaining. It doesn't take you as many words."

Lord, thank you that we are all important to you. Help us see one another as you see us. Amen.

A Quiet Place

In the morning, while it was still very dark, [Jesus] got up and went out to a deserted place, and there he prayed (Mark 1:35).

*O*NE OF THE UNDERGRADUATE COLLEGES I ATTENDED was Atlantic Christian College (today Barton College) in Wilson, North Carolina. The religion department there was topnotch. One of my professors, William Paulsell, introduced me to the great mystics of the church and the importance of nurturing my spiritual life. Out of this kind of concern, the religion students of the college, with the support of the faculty, built a small round building on the campus that was named, "The Still Point." The simple building in a quiet part of the campus had cushions for kneeling or lying down. It was an oasis of quietness and stillness in what sometimes got to be a desert of stress and strain. I often went to that quiet place to seek the still point in my heart. Almost always I left refreshed and ready to take on whatever tasks presented themselves.

Jesus also often sought out a quiet place, a still

point, a place where he could commune with God without distractions (Mark 1:35; 6:30-32). If Jesus needed to visit a quiet place frequently, how much more do you and I?

Quiet places are hard to find, aren't they? Our world is so loud and busy. We have so many pressures on us, so many things to do, so many people wanting things from us. That was not foreign to Jesus either. He had to get up while it was still dark and go away to find his quiet place, but even then he was interrupted.

Still, we need to find the time and place to be with God. There we can get away from the noise and focus once again on God, on who we are, and on what we are all about. Finding quiet places and times to commune with God provides light for our path, rest from our hectic pace, and renewed strength for service.

What should we do in the quiet place?

We can pray; we can pour our heart out to God. That's important. But most often I just sit in silence in my quiet place, listening for God to speak to me. Indeed, the best part of finding a quiet place is that you begin to hone your sense of God's presence. The Bible and Christian testimony throughout the centuries reveal that God is not just found in the spectacular, the Pentecost-like experiences, but also in stillness and quiet.

When the prophet Elijah was running away from Ahab and Jezebel, he hid in a cave. There he listened for God in an earthquake, in a mighty wind, and in fire but heard nothing. It was in a "sound of sheer silence" that he finally met God (1 Kings 19:11-12). Sometimes we have to go to a cave or, like Jesus, get away from it all in order to be able to hear God. If we do that often enough, then it becomes easier even in the noisy, busy world to filter out everything else so we can hear God.

My soul, wait in silence for God; for my expectation is from God. Amen.

A Prayer With Names in It

Are any among you sick? They should call for the elders of the church and have them pray over them, anointing them with oil in the name of the Lord. . . . The prayer of the righteous is powerful and effective (James 5:14, 16b).

ONCE I RECEIVED AN E-MAIL FROM A FRIEND IN Florida. Her name is Cyndy, and she had been very sick. She began by saying to those on her mailing list: "You guys have been praying again, haven't you?" Then she went on to tell how, though she had not slept well, she woke up singing, "It's a Beautiful Morning. . . ." She attributed this sense of wellness to the prayers of her circle of friends.

Soon afterward I was leaving a home where relatives were gathered after the death of a family member. As I passed a group of mourners on the front porch, I stopped to ask for prayers for myself and others; for there had been several deaths connected to our church over a two-week period. After I made the request, I was about to leave when they stopped me. "No time like the present, Bass," they said to me. So, this circle of friends held hands with me; and I bathed in the warmth, inspiration, and strength of their prayers right there on the front porch.

Sometime later I received the following card from dear friends:

"Each week we choose someone from our friends and family to pray for during the week. This week we'll be remembering you. We'll pray for you as an individual, a couple, and a family. We'll be praying for your church and for your spiritual, emotional, financial, and physical needs. We think of you and the family often. Hope things are going OK for you. Love, John and Jane"

Again I was reminded of just how important prayer is, especially praying for others. Such intercessory prayer is prayer with names in it— names of family, friends, maybe even people you don't know, maybe even your own name.

Once I had been invited to go to California to work with some people from Laos called Hmongs. I agreed to go, but I was nervous. I had never been on an airplane and never been that far from home. The people of my church, the Sunday before I was to leave, called me to the altar. There I knelt and the whole church gathered around me, many resting their hands on my head and shoulder, while they prayed for me. I tell you, I felt the presence and power of God in a way that day that I never had before. I stood up encouraged and empowered.

How should we pray for others? Let me share a way taught to me by one of my childhood church school teachers. "Praying for others is as simple as looking at the five fingers on your hand," she said. "Your thumb is nearest to you, so begin your prayers by praying for those closest to you. Your family, your friends."

"The next finger is the pointing finger. Pray for those who teach, instruct, and heal. This includes teachers, doctors, and ministers."

"The next finger is the tallest figure. It reminds us of our leaders. Pray for the president, leaders in industry, and administrators. Also for world leaders, even our enemies. What they do influences us all."

"The fourth finger is our ring finger. Surprising to many is the fact that this is our weakest finger, as most piano teachers will tell you. It reminds us to pray for those who are weak, in trouble, or in pain."

"And last comes our little finger, the smallest of all, which is where we should put ourselves in relation to God and others. As the Bible says, 'The least shall be the greatest among you.' Your pinkie should remind you to pray for yourself."

Many Christians seem to think that they have no particular gift for ministry in the church. Perhaps you feel that way. But there is a ministry, a vital one that all of us can have, that can have a tremendous impact on your church and whole community. It's the ministry of intercessory prayer, and that's just prayer with names in it.

Loving God, you do not mind us praying to you about ourselves. But you also like to hear the names of other people, too, when we pray. Help us remember to think of others when we pray. In so doing perhaps you might use us, our words, our hands to reach out to them. Amen.

Turn on the Light!

Thy word is a lamp unto my feet, and a light unto my path (Psalm 119:105, KJV).

HOW WELL I REMEMBER IT. MY TOE STILL STINGS. The phone was ringing in the middle of the night. It should have been on the table beside my bed, but we have a portable phone that's never where it should be. In fact, it has a little button on the base unit that makes it ring so you can find it. Without that button, the phone would have been lost forever long ago. So there I was stumbling in the dark looking for it, only to stump my toe and end up hopping on one foot, holding the other, throbbing foot in both hands. Then, out of the darkness, the voice of wisdom came, "Why don't you turn on the light?"

That experience made me reflect on the Bible and how the psalmist found God's Word to be a great light for him.

Turning on a light is a simple thing to do. You

find the switch and turn it to ON. If you've paid your electricity bill and do not have a bad bulb, you should have light.

For God's Word to be a light, we must turn it on. We do that by opening and reading the Bible. It's that simple.

I had a ceiling light and a lamp on the desk in my bedroom that night when the phone rang, but they did me no good at all until I switched them on. In the Bible, we have a wondrous light for our dark paths; but it does us no good until we open it, read it, turn it on.

The Bible only becomes a light when we give it a fresh hearing. In other words, each time we read the Bible or hear it read, we can try to act as if that is the first time we have read or heard the words. Sometimes we do not really hear the Bible or receive the light it has to give because we think we already know what's there. We have preconceived notions about what the words mean, so we do not really give them a fresh hearing.

I have a comic strip that shows a young man reading his Bible as his sister comes by. He says to her, "Don't bother me. I'm looking up verses to back up my preconceived notions."

Most of us have been guilty of doing just that—going to the Bible, not to hear what it has to say, but to find support for that which we already believe or have made up our minds about. There is nothing wrong with going to the Bible with our questions and concerns. But when we do, we need to listen for its answers, not impose on it what we want it to say.

The biblical writers are not here to defend themselves, to say, "Hold it! That's not what I meant!" So we have to be very careful to listen and to concentrate in order to hear what the Bible really has to say. James tells us not to be just hearers of the word but "doers of the word" as well (James 1:22). If the Bible is to become light for us, it must also become part of our lives, influencing and guiding us.

Once I went to my doctor about a medical problem. Tests were run, and it was discovered that I have a hernia. She then told me things I could do to help deal with this problem, foods to eat, and so forth. I made a wise decision to go to the doctor, for she possessed the knowledge I needed. Now it would be foolish of me to ignore her instructions. How foolish of us, too, to turn on the light of God's Word but then not follow it— to choose instead to stumble back into the darkness.

One Christmas my daughter received a complex dollhouse. When I tried to assemble it for her, I got it all wrong. Clearly I was frustrated, and Meredith noticed this. In the midst of my fumbling darkness, her voice of reason filled the air: "Daddy, here are the instructions. Why don't you use them?"

The psalmist says God's Word is a lamp for our feet, not a search beam that shows all the way down the path. God's guidance often comes to us in enough light for a few steps so that we walk by faith, not by sight. We are not promised that we can see every rock in the path or that we will never stump our toe, or take a wrong turn, or even stumble and fall. But this lamp will give us light enough to get back up and keep walking.

Oh, by the way, I solved the problem of looking for the phone in the dark. No, I didn't unplug it (though that's always a possibility). We got a nightlight. Not much to it. Just a tiny bulb you plug into the wall. It gets the job done, however. You would be surprised at how much difference that little light makes when it's dark and you can't see your way.

It seems to me that is exactly what the psalmist is telling us. God's Word is a lamp for your feet and light for your path. Why stumble along in the dark? Keep reading it. Keep studying it. Keep meditating on it. Let it shine on your path each day and follow it. Turn on the light and keep it on.

Lord, O how I love your Word. It is my meditation all the day and night. Amen.

Valentines From God

I have called you by name, you are mine....
I will be with you....Because you are
precious in my sight, and honored, and I
love you (Isaiah 43:1, 2, 4).

I WAS IN WAL-MART ONE FEBRUARY AND WALKED BY the Valentine's Day card section. There were cards of every size, shape, and color. Some were simple and others ornate. There was a valentine for everyone, not just for your sweetheart, but for all the persons you love.

As I stood there looking at all those cards and the people buying them to give to family and friends, the thought came to me, *God sends valentines too.* Valentines are messages of love, right? Who loves more than God? Each of us is God's beloved. Every day is Valentine's Day, for God showers love upon us every second of our lives.

Take a breath. Every breath is a valentine from God. Every sunrise, sunset, starry sky; every meal, walk, hug from a friend. Every second of our lives is filled with valentines, with an "I Love You" from God.

The Bible is a collection of the most wonderful valentines ever written or given. Here are love letters from God to you and to me for us to read over and over, to cherish, and to find reassurance that we are loved.

I have loved you with an everlasting love;
therefore I have continued my faithfulness to
you (Jeremiah 31:3).

[God's] banner over me was love
(Song of Solomon 2:4, KJV).

Though the mountains leave their place
and the hills be shaken,
My love shall never leave you
nor my covenant of peace be shaken,
says the LORD, who has mercy on you
(Isaiah 54:10, NAB).

O Lord, how precious is your love. My God,
the children of the earth find refuge in the shelter
of your wings
(Psalm 36:7, author's paraphrase of New Revised Standard Version).

Your love and loyalty will always keep me safe
(Psalm 40:11b, TEV).

But I trusted in your steadfast love;
  my heart shall rejoice in your salvation.
I will sing to the LORD,
  because he has dealt bountifully with me
(Psalm 13:5-6).

The LORD came to my support.
He set me free in the open,
  and rescued me, because he loves me
(Psalm 18:19-20, NAB).

I trust in you.
I will be glad and rejoice
  because of your constant love
(Psalm 31:6-7, TEV).

Because your steadfast love is better than life,
  my lips will praise you (Psalm 63:3).

But you, O Lord, are a God merciful and gracious,
  slow to anger and abounding in steadfast love
  and faithfulness (Psalm 86:15).

See how much the Father has loved us! His love is so great that we are called God's children—and so, in fact, we are (1 John 3:1, TEV).

We have known and believe the love that God has for us. God is love, and those who abide in love abide in God, and God abides in them (1 John 4:16).

We love because God first loved us (1 John 4:19, TEV).

Who shall separate us from the love of Christ? shall tribulation, or distress, or persecution, or famine, or nakedness, or peril, or sword? . . . . Nay, in all these things we are more than conquerors through him that loved us. For I am persuaded, that neither death, nor life, nor angels, nor principalities, nor powers, nor things present, nor things to come, [n]or height, nor depth, nor any other creature, shall be able to separate us from the love of God, which is in Christ Jesus our Lord (Romans 8:35, 37-39, KJV).

Many people do not just send a card on Valentine's Day. They send gifts like flowers or a box of candy. God was not satisfied with just cards either, just words on paper. No. God gave us all the best, the sweetest, the most wondrous gift of all:

For God so loved the world, that he gave his only begotten Son, that whosoever believeth in him should not perish, but have everlasting life (John 3:16, KJV).

The Word became flesh,
and made his dwelling among us,
and we have seen his glory:

the glory of an only Son coming from the Father,
filled with enduring love.... Of his fullness
we have all had a share—
love following upon love
(John 1:14, 16, NAB).

This greatest of all Valentines comes from the very heart of God, overflowing with love, grace, mercy, forgiveness, and life abundant and eternal.

I remember the first time we gave out valentines in elementary school. You could give them to whomever you wished. That was good for some people, the most popular ones; for they received more valentines than anyone else. Others got a few. Some did not get any at all. Well, the next year the teacher changed things so that each person gave every other person in the class a valentine.

Valentines from God are not just for a few. They are for you, me, everyone, every day of the year. For each day is Valentine's Day when you are the beloved of God.

May Christ dwell in your hearts through faith; that you, being rooted and grounded in love, may have power to comprehend with all the saints what is the breadth and length and height and depth, and to know the love of Christ which surpasses knowledge, that you may be filled with all the fullness of God. Amen (Ephesians 3:17-20, author's paraphrase of New Revised Standard Version).

Magnets

When I am lifted up from the earth, I will draw everyone to me (John 12:32, TEV).

I HAVE ALWAYS BEEN FASCINATED BY MAGNETS. Magnets create some wondrous, mysterious force that draws certain metals to them. I remember learning about magnets in school. We had lots of little particles of iron in a jar of sand. Trying to pick each of them out by hand with some tweezers would have taken forever. So guess what we did? We used a magnet. When one of us held the magnet over the sand, hundreds of those tiny iron particles came wiggling through the sand and stuck to that magnet.

I cannot help but remember that experiment when I read in John that Jesus spoke of being lifted up and drawing people to himself. There was something magnetic about Jesus. From his birth, he attracted people from all walks of life—from lowly shepherds to the learned magi, from the elderly in the Temple (Simeon and Anna) to little children, from tax collectors to fishermen, from a Pharisee who came in the night (Nicodemus) to one who would destroy Christians at first (Saul), from people of all nations (Pentecost). When Jesus was lifted up on the cross, his arms stretched out, a powerful drawing force was let loose in the world. Its magnetism is so powerful that it spans time to reach out and draw people in every generation.

In John 12:20-21, we see how some Greeks, Gentiles, were drawn to Jesus. They asked Philip, one of Jesus' disciples, "Sir, we wish to see Jesus." Here is a foreshadow of what was to come—that Jesus, lifted up on the cross, exalted by the Resurrection and Ascension, would be lifted up by Paul, Peter, and countless others so that the Gentiles would be drawn to Christ and into God's kingdom. These men were the first outsiders of countless millions to be drawn to Christ.

A friend shared with me a conversation she had with her twenty-year-old son. In it, he told her, "I keep trying to be an atheist, but Jesus keeps drawing me back!"

A college student once told me much the same thing: "The strange thing about Jesus is that you can never get away from him."

There is something about Jesus...something magnetic that draws us to him...that will not let us go. This mysterious, magnetic force flowing from the "lifted up" Christ is the love of God.

When a piece of metal, like a paper clip, is attached to a magnet, the paper clip also becomes a magnet. (Some metals, if attached to magnetic forces long enough, become magnetized them-selves—permanently.) What do you think hap-pens when the paper clip attached to a magnet comes into contact with another paper clip? If the original magnet is strong enough, that paper clip draws others until you have a long stream of paper clips.

That is the goal of my life—to be so close to Christ that others are drawn to him through me. Is it your goal too?

I cannot stand, loving Lord, at the foot of Golgotha without my eyes being compelled to look up. There, on the face of Christ, I see you, your love, just how far you would go to let me and your world know the depth of your love. No matter where I go, no matter how far I may wander from the cross, I still feel the pull of your love. I yield, Lord. I yield. Amen.

The Right Helper

For while we were still weak, at the right time
Christ died for the ungodly (Romans 5:6).

ONE OF THE MOST IMPORTANT INSIGHTS I HAVE learned about the Christian life is profound yet simple. It has increased my understanding of how God works in our lives, helped me grow in my spiritual life, and brought me a great deal of comfort and peace. That insight is simply this: Often God guides and helps us by giving us a person, a helper, the right helper at just the right time in our lives.

The greatest blessings God gives are not possessions but persons. The most meaningful experiences in life come through the relationships we have with these special persons, those right helpers God sends our way just when we need them.

The Bible is the story of how God has always provided the right helper at the right time. Whenever God wanted to truly bless God's people, God did not send them things. God sent a person. A helper.

We see this process happening as early as the

second chapter of the Bible. God makes Adam and Adam is lonely. God says, "It is not good that the man should be alone; I will make him an help meet for him" (Genesis 2:18, KJV). First Adam looks among the animals of the world to find a companion. I've often wondered what he said when the elephant and giraffe were created. Probably, "Lord, no! This just isn't going to work." So, God makes Adam fall asleep and creates woman from Adam's rib. I like the way *The Living Bible* paraphrases Adam's first words when he sees Eve, "Wow! This is it!" God has been doing the same for Adams and Eves ever since.

When the Hebrews are languishing in Egyptian slavery, crying out to God for deliverance, what does God do? God sends them the right helper at the right time—Moses.

When the people, settled in the Promised Land, face a crisis from their enemies, what does God do? God raises up judges—Othniel, Ehud, Deborah, Gideon, Samson—helpers, the right helpers at just the right time.

When the nation is moving away from God toward certain destruction, what does God do? God sends them prophets—Amos, Hosea, Jeremiah, and many more—the right helpers at the right time.

When this world is at its weakest and most needy, what does God do? God sends the greatest helper of all—just at the right time—Jesus.

The whole biblical story is about how God sends the right helpers at the right times. And you know what? That is also the story of my life and yours.

God has just kept sending helpers into my life—teachers, coaches, youth leaders, friends, ministers, a loving wife who has helped me more than I can say. I have come to rely on this help and to live in anticipation of just who God's going to send into my life next just when I need him or her.

It was the very first week of my very first pastorate at a small church in Colquitt, Georgia. A member of the church had died, and I was expected to conduct the funeral. I had never done that before. I was extremely nervous and unsure about what to do. But God sent me the right helper at the right time. The family asked me if Reverend Aycock, another local minister, could assist me. Little did they know that I would be the one doing the assisting. Reverend Aycock, an older and much more experienced minister, listened as I told him my dilemma. He showed great patience and understanding. He told me exactly what to do. The service went well.

Remember the story of Helen Keller, the young girl who had a high fever that robbed her of her sight and hearing? What would have become of this little girl, living in a silent, dark world, had God not sent her the right helper at the right time—a woman named Anne Sullivan?

You see, we are all Helen Kellers. We all need help of one kind or another. No one is totally independent and self-sufficient. We may be too stubborn or proud to admit that we need help, but we need it nonetheless. So, God sends into our lives our own Anne Sullivans, those special helpers just when we need them who make all the difference.

Jesus was the greatest of all God's helpers. He spent his life helping people. He was the right helper at the right time for the woman at the well, who was thirsting for spiritual wholeness. I don't think it was an accident that he just happened to be there at noon that day when she came for water. Look wherever you will in the Gospels, Jesus was the right helper at the right time for so many.

The good news is that Jesus went on to the cross and thereby became the right helper for the whole world. Millions throughout history have found in him a helper unlike any other—a helper who gives a saving, healing, forgiving love that transforms their whole lives.

Give thanks for him and remember the names of those other right helpers God has given you at the right time. Draw encouragement from this truth: God has always given you the right helper at the right time in the past. God will not stop now. Just when you need help, God will provide just the right helper. Maybe too God is waiting to use you as the right helper at the right time for someone else.

O Greatest of Helpers, thank you for all the right helpers you have given me at the right time, especially Jesus. If it be your will, use me as the right helper at the right time for others. Amen.

The Sparrow

As [Jesus] was walking along, he saw Levi son of Alphaeus sitting at the tax booth, and he said to him, "Follow me" (Mark 2:14).

WE HAVE A LARGE BIRD FEEDER HANGING FROM the edge of our front porch, along with a red feeder full of liquid sugar water for hummingbirds. One of the little joys of my day is sitting quietly on the front porch and watching the birds. We have to refill the feeder just about every day because so many birds visit it. They congregate in small trees that line our driveway where it's only a ten-foot flight to the feeders. Every kind of bird, every size and color, shows up every day. By far, however, the sparrows outnumber the rest. It's common to see the whole feeder covered with their little, brown feathery bodies. Others sit on top of the feeder waiting their turn or walk around on the ground beneath picking up fallen seed.

Today I noticed one particular sparrow. This little sparrow had dark brown V-shaped color on its breast just below the beak. I believe it's called an English sparrow but confess to not being a bird expert. This little sparrow was not eating the seed but filling its beak with seed and then flying back to a branch in a tree. I saw another sparrow hop up to it on the branch, a sparrow that looked fully grown but sickly. Perhaps it had had a run-in with a cat since some of the feathers on its head were missing. The first sparrow was flying back and forth from the feeder feeding the sickly one, placing the seed right in its beak. I watched in awe and respect as this went on for some time. This sparrow even protected the hurt sparrow when some other birds tried to attack it. He puffed up his feathers and stood his ground. I had to leave to take care of an errand. When I came back, I saw both sparrows sitting on the branch, side by side, seemingly taking an afternoon nap.

I thought of all the people who had been like that kind sparrow for me when I was hurting and not able to feed myself. I thought of their count-less unselfish acts and words of encouragement and nourishment. I gave thanks to God for them. Then I thought of other "little sparrows"—wounded, frightened souls who just need some-one to notice, someone to care enough to offer a seed or two, or someone to just sit beside them for a while.

To all outward appearances, Levi had it made. He was wealthy. But I do not think he was happy. How could he be happy when everyone hated him, saw him as a traitor, would gladly do him in, like those birds were trying to do to the hurt one? Levi was an outsider, a sinner, an outcast; and he knew it. He was reminded of it every day. He was never invited to anyone's home, anyone respectable that is. No one ever looked on him with anything but hatred...until the Bird Watcher came by that day, the one with such kind eyes and a gentle voice. "Follow me," he said. "Come, be with me. Eat at my table. I will be your friend."

One of the first things Levi did was take Jesus around to his wounded, hungry friends, persons not invited to God's table by the religious powers that be. The eyes of Jesus were always on the outer branches, to see the shining eyes and hungering souls, tax collectors and sinners as far from the bird feeder as anyone could be. He fed them. He welcomed them. He sat and ate with them. He fearlessly defended them. Then Jesus gave his life on a tree for all us little sparrows.

Who has healed and fed you when you were most in need? Is there a little sparrow who needs you?

Lord, when we kneel at your table and the bread is placed in our mouths, we gladly take it. We do nothing to earn it and can do nothing. We don't have to, for you just give it freely. The bread is for us a visible sign of all your blessings, more than we can count. It is as if, Lord, you spend your every moment taking from the riches of your bird feeder and feeding us with grace, love, peace, acceptance, healing, and best of all communion with you. We thank you for those you have used to help feed us when we were unable to do so for ourselves, unable or just didn't care, or had given up on ourselves and perhaps also on you. Your lovingkindness keeps us alive. Let us be your helpers, too, scanning the branches around us for the little wounded ones, the ones left out, who can't make it to the feeder. Help us never to be so busy that we cannot also just sit there with them, napping, chatting, being there; for they hunger for that as much as anything. Fill our days with praises for you and your bounty and for the assurance that your eye is always on each sparrow, even on us. Amen.

Table Talk

*When he was at the table with them, he took
bread, blessed and broke it, and gave it to
them. Then their eyes were opened, and they
recognized him (Luke 24:30-31).*

"WHAT STANDS OUT IN YOUR MEMORY FROM
when you were growing up?" a seminar leader
asked us once.

You know what came to mind for me? Meals. I
don't know about your family, but my family was
into eating. Usually it was Sunday dinner. And it
wasn't just my immediate family but uncles,
aunts, grandparents, cousins, even some people
only distantly, if at all, related to us. We'd gather
at grandmother's house, turning her yard into a
used car lot. The women gathered in the kitchen
or living room and the men on the front porch.
All the cousins were running around in the yard
playing games. But it all stopped when we heard
the dinner bell ringing. We gathered around the
tables and one of the grownups said grace, which
always seemed to last a lot longer than I thought
it should. Then we would eat. And the only sound

you would hear for a while was the clanging of forks, knives, pots, and plates. But soon the table talk began. Someone would start telling a story about the last time we were together or about something that happened to one of our ancestors. When I close my eyes, I can still see their faces— Aunt Alma, Uncle Vance, Grandfather Wells, Cousin Lee....I learned a lot about them and myself from those table talks. There's just something special about eating together.

You know, some of the best memories of my home church in Bridgeton, North Carolina, are the meals we had together. I remember Mr. Roy who always made the coffee and how Junior (I don't remember his last name) made a sign to put on the pot—"Drink at Your own Risk." And the fish stews the men had and invited me. And then there were all the church barbecues and the covered dish dinners. The women were usually in the kitchen and the men setting up tables or sitting around in clusters of chairs engaged in guy talk (it did not occur to them in those days that it was OK for them also to be in the kitchen). And the children, my cousins in the faith, were running around in the churchyard having a ball...until the dinner bell rang. And the preacher led us in the blessing, which was also way too long to me, and then we'd eat. And there would be a short time of silence as everyone began, but it soon turned into lots of table talk. As I listened, I heard many stories that disclosed who these people were and who I was, too. There's just something special about eating together.

The churches I know that seem vibrant are the ones that spend time around the table. Eating together creates and strengthens bonds. Breaking bread together breaks down the barriers that separate us, helping us come together. There's something about eating together that helps remove the masks we use to hide who we are. Our eyes are opened to really see one another.

I think meals are so special and important because they are about the only time we take to sit down long enough in someone's presence so that we can talk. We need that as much as we need food. We need to talk about our day, to tell stories, to get to know one another better. There's something about eating together that helps that happen.

I meet each week with some of the other ministers in the area to study the Bible and pray. After the meeting, we usually gather at the Country Café, a local restaurant, to eat—a Roman Catholic priest, two Presbyterian ministers, two United Methodist pastors (one a former Baptist). Sounds like a recipe for indigestion, you may be thinking. But you know what? As good as those Bible and prayer times are, it's the meals I enjoy the most; for I have really gotten to know and care for these ministers of God through breaking bread together, and they have gotten to know me.

GOD SIGHTINGS

The story of the Emmaus Road is one of my
favorites (Luke 24:13-35). Cleopas and his travel-
ing companion did not recognize Jesus when they
walked with him for hours. They didn't even realize who he was when he was expounding the
Scriptures to them, although they had this
strange warming glow inside as he talked. It was
only when he broke the bread at mealtime that
they really saw him. There is something special
about eating together.

Is it not interesting that at a central place in
each sanctuary is a table? (Some call it an altar.)
For at the heart of the Christian faith is a meal—
the Lord's Supper—the Holy Communion, the
Eucharist, and the Mass. When Jesus wanted to
give us a gift, he gave us a meal, for he knew that
there was something special about meals, about
eating together. In the context of his supper we
are reminded about who he was, what he did for
us, that he is even now present with us. Through
the breaking of that bread, he is disclosed to our
blinded eyes, too. There's something special
about eating together.

The early church knew this. Acts 2:42 says that
one of the things the early Christians devoted
themselves to was "the breaking of bread" and
fellowship. They ate together as often as possible.
And often during those meals they observed the
Lord's Supper. And it wasn't a solemn, funeral-
like observance for them. It was a celebration of

96

a risen, living Lord! It was a joyous family meal filled with lots of table talk.

Great and Good Host, you not only save us a place at your table and serve the most bountiful and delicious food, you also provide us with the most delightful table talk. Help us to be better listeners and talkers so that we might come to know You and one another better, as we sit around Your table. Amen.

"A Table for One, Please"

[Jesus] withdrew from there in a boat to a deserted place by himself. But when the crowds heard it, they followed him on foot from the towns. When he went ashore, he saw a great crowd (Matthew 14:13-14).

I HAVE HAD SEVERAL EXPERIENCES LATELY THAT I want to share with you. Maybe, just maybe, God's been trying to teach me something.

The first one came while on vacation. We stopped in Amish Country (Lancaster County, Pennsylvania) and ate at the Plain and Fancy Restaurant. We were expecting to sit at a table by ourselves, just my family, us four and no more. Well, seems that's not the way they do it there. We sat at a huge table with several other families; and we had to eat family style, that is, pass everything. So, instead of being able to just sit by ourselves, we were forced into community, into sharing. We met and got to know some families we never would have otherwise. It was like a true family gathering as we laughed and told things about ourselves. (The oldest man at the table, kind of a grandfather figure, even gave my kids a dollar when we left.) If it's a table for one or just for your own family you want, you don't want to eat there. That's not how they do things at the Plain and Fancy.

The second experience took place at a wedding rehearsal dinner at which my wife and I did not know anyone (except the couple being married). A room in the Country Café, a popular local restaurant, was reserved with one long table in the middle and several small, more private ones on the side. Not knowing anyone and not really wishing to, my wife and I sat at one of the tables to the side.

Well, the mother of the groom would have none of that (perhaps she once worked at the Plain and Fancy). She insisted that we move to the middle table, right in the midst of a bunch of people we did not know. I was forced to sit beside a grand-mother who had been through three husbands, whom she told me about in detail. She kept say-ing how nice it was to sit beside such a handsome young man. On the other side was the latest addi-tion to the family—a noisy, overly plump infant in a highchair who made really weird sounds with each spoonful of food shoveled into his mouth. My wife, Debbie, did not fare much better. She sat between the groom's father and his brother. We both looked longingly at the table we had just left, so appealing, so lovely, so lonely in the corner.

Then things started to change. We began talking, getting to know this family, and they us. I began to like them, to feel comfortable with them. There was a real sense of family there that would not have been possible had we been left at our own little table in the corner. In fact, because of that dinner together, several of the members of the family have come by to talk with me about personal problems. I guess they began to trust me. This is a family in which there are no tables for one or two. That's not how they do things.

Then, I went by a local store, got the *Roanoke Times* and *Washington Post*, and headed for Covington for a couple of worry-free, relaxing hours at a table for one in Hardee's. Before I even got to my table, two persons I had seen before but did not really know came up to me and said, "Hello! How about some company?"

"Sure," I replied, trying to keep from sobbing in my decaf.

This couple, maybe in their sixties, sat down at my table, MY TABLE. I kind-of resented it. I was looking forward to being alone. But, no, God's got a sense of humor and an even greater sense of community. For before long the newspapers were set aside, and I was engaged in a most enjoyable conversation with the couple. I had a strange feeling at one point that this was what it would be like to sit down with my parents, if I could, and just talk. (My father died several years ago.) The man, about six feet tall with thinning gray hair, even reminded me of my dad (he, too, was a carpenter). No table for one that day. And I was glad.

The following Sunday was World Communion Sunday. During the service I kept thinking that God's restaurant is a Plain and Fancy one. There are no tables for one or for just one family. The Lord's table is for the whole family... even ones I do not know are in the family. When we sit and eat together, something special, something wondrous happens. We start to feel like a family. We begin to talk, to get to know one another. The Lord's table is one very long table that circles the world. So, if it's a table for one or for just your own family you're looking for here, you're in the wrong place. That's not how we do things here.

Lord, like you, may everyone find me welcoming and inviting. Help me to understand how very special it is to sit and eat with others, especially at your table. Amen.

This Is Not My House

As he sat at dinner in the house, many tax collectors and sinners came and were sitting with him and his disciples (Matthew 9:10).

*T*HIS IS NOT MY HOUSE.
This is God's house.
I cannot tell God
who is welcome and who is not.

This is not my table.
I do not sit at the head as host.
It is the table of Christ. He is Host.
I cannot tell the Host
who can sit here and who cannot.

This is not my food on this sacred table.
I did not prepare it. It is not my blood, my body.
It is the very life of the Christ laid out here.
I cannot tell Him, this One who constantly
ate with sinners, who is worthy to partake of it
and who is not.

The doors of God's house are open to
all who need shelter, who crave the fellowship
and friendship of God, and even to those who
hate God or cannot bring themselves to trust that
God exists or could care for them. Anyone, everyone
is welcome as honored guests in God's house.

This table of Christ is long and it has many chairs.
There is always room for one more,
for those craving the fellowship of the sacred
   table,
a place to belong,
to be somebody to Somebody.
Anyone, everyone has a place at the table of
   Christ.

This food, simple yet divine, is bountiful, abundant, ample for all,
especially those who are hungry and thirsty for
   what
mere bread and drink cannot supply.
Anyone, everyone has a plate and a portion
served by the very hand of the Christ.
No one is sent away hungry or thirsty here.

Lord, who am I that you swing open your door
   and embrace me?
Who am I that you escort me to your table and
   pull out a chair for me?

Who am I that you would provide such wondrous
and costly food?
How can I but humbly bow my head at such
grace?

So, Lord, help me be like you—embracing all
your guests, all who,
like me, are unworthy of your house, unfit for
your table and food,
yet are welcomed, seated, and fed anyway.

*Lord, I see the door open, a chair pulled out for
me, a plate set for me. Not only for me, Lord, for all
your children. Amen.*

From Walls
to Bridges

*Everyone will know that you are my disciples,
if you have love for one another (John 13:35).*

*Some people from Chloe's family have told me
quite plainly, my friends, that there are quar-
rels among you (1 Corinthians 1:11, TEV).*

I LOOK ON HELPLESSLY AS THE BOARDS GO UP,
the hammers pound nail after nail,
creating walls—tall, wide, thick walls...

And I see them growing alienated, estranged,
separate from one another, not being able or will-
    ing
to see or hear one another, and wondering why...

And the anger grows, the misunderstanding fes-
    ters like a wound,
and they stay behind their walls, aching deep
    inside
but not sure why or what to do about it...

Such walls, hated things, monstrous creations
    that
we make with our own hands of malice, hearts
    callous,
minds prejudiced, eyes judging, ears sealed . . .

Who can deliver us from these walls? What could
possibly break through them? Trapped. Impris-
    oned. Lonely. Aching.
Afraid. Broken. Alone . . . Are these walls eternal?

And then, suddenly, there is a new sound.
Not hammering. Not of another board, or brick.
No, a steady tapping against the walls . . .

And it will not stop. It will not cease, this tapping,
this chipping away at the walls. For this tapping
    is
someone's confession, of taking responsibility for
    being a wall builder . . .

And suddenly there is another tapping, that
    begins to shake
the walls . . . it is an apology . . . little words, tiny
    whispers cast against the
massive walls . . . "I'm sorry . . . It's my fault . . . I was
    wrong . . ."

And then the walls tremble, another force, more
    powerful

than the other two, slams against them—"I for-
    give you . . ."
forgiveness joins the fray, tumbling the walls to
    pieces,
smashing through them as mere paper . . .

And wonder of wonders, these three, this holy
    trinity—
confession, apology, forgiveness—pick up shat-
    tered walls—
bricks, cement, steel, and wood, and transform
    them into bridges . . .

And tentatively at first they take a step on those
    bridges,
a step toward one another, and suddenly they see
    one another
again, feel their own hearts yearning, needing the
    other . . .

And the pace quickens, eyes embrace, smiles
    radiate,
arms encircle, hearts mingle, hands held, memo-
    ries of the walls
fade away in the joy of standing on the bridges of
    reconciliation.

*Dear God, sometimes we build such thick walls
around us, shutting out others, even maybe you.
And we have reinforced them for so long that we*

wonder if they can ever be brought down. Lord, give us the tools of confession, apology, and forgiveness. Teach us how to use them so that the walls begin to quake and crumble, and help us in their ruins to construct bridges. Amen.

The Orchestra

For just as the body is one and has many members, and all the members of the body, though many, are one body, so it is with Christ. For in the one Spirit we were all baptized into one body—Jews or Greeks, slaves or free—and we were all made to drink of one Spirit. Indeed, the body does not consist of one member but of many (1 Corinthians 12:12-14).

I GREW UP IN EASTERN NORTH CAROLINA AND attended Bridgeton Elementary School for eight years. Bridgeton is a small town across the Neuse River from New Bern, North Carolina. During my eighth-grade year, our class went over to the high school auditorium one day to hear the North Carolina Symphony. We sat about midway back in the auditorium. Janitors were busily cleaning up some aisles. Ushers made sure we got in the right seats. Others gave us brochures that told all about the orchestra and the program for that day. The orchestra was hidden behind a velvet maroon curtain. We could hear them warming up, tuning their instruments, a sound I had never heard before.

Suddenly, the curtains opened and there on the stage were men and women dressed in black. I noticed several nationalities among them. They sat in sections—strings, wind instruments, brass, percussion. I saw many different kinds of instruments I had never seen before and could not identify. I remember pondering how all these people could play their instruments together without it sounding like chaos.

The conductor walked out on the stage, gray haired, tall, and slender. He was wearing a black formal suit with the coat partly split up the back. He stepped up onto a small platform, adjusting a small podium or music stand on which rested a thick book. The conductor opened the book, looked around at all the orchestra members, tapped his baton on the metal stand, raised the baton into the air, and all together the persons in the orchestra readied their instruments as if they were one. They played the "Fugue" from Britten's "Young Person's Guide to the Orchestra." The sweet sound of the flutes came first, then the piccolo, oboes, clarinets, bassoons, violins, violas, cellos, double basses, harp, horns, trumpets, trombones, bass tuba, and percussion—the full orchestra. The beauty and magnificence of the sound of all those instruments took my breath away. My life was changed that day by the glorious sounds of the symphony.

I have come to realize that the church is an orchestra too. It has one Conductor, many musicians, and many instruments. Each has been given a different musical gift to contribute and a different part to play. Like an orchestra, there are persons who set up the stage, who act as ushers in the auditorium, who advertise, and who do many other things. All of them are as important as anyone else. Each needs the other. Though we have different parts to play, if we stop and listen to one another, we will discover that we are playing the same symphony and are directed by the same Conductor. When we play together, instead of just our own part in our own little section, we make music so glorious, so moving that it can touch and transform the world.

Great Conductor, what an honor you bestow on each of us, asking us to play in your orchestra. Help us to value one another and to always keep our eyes on you, that together we might blend as one in the wondrous symphony of your good news. Amen.

"Damaged Goods
... Cheap"

For you were bought with a price
(1 Corinthians 6:20).

ONE OF MY FIRST REAL JOBS WAS IN A GROCERY store. I started out as a bag boy but soon was promoted—given my own aisle to stock. Trucks brought in hundreds of boxes of food every week, and we had to unpack them and put the stock on the shelves. Almost every week, however, we would open a box and find that some of the cans or cartons had been damaged. For example, some cans had lost their labels, had dents, or were crushed so badly that a portion of the contents had spilled out.

We were told by the manager not to put these cans on the shelves because no one would buy them. So, we often would place some of them in a basket in the front of the store. On the basket was a large sign that read, "Damaged Goods. Cheap." Still not very many people bought the damaged goods. Most just ignored them. Often we ended up sending the cans back to the manufacturers.

One day, I happened to notice a woman being interviewed on television. She had been through a lot of tough times—divorced, unemployed, a single parent. When the reporter asked about her love life, she answered, "I look at myself as damaged goods. Nobody wants damaged goods."

I could not help but think about Jesus and the woman at the well (John 4) and wonder if perhaps she felt like "damaged goods." She was a Samaritan, a woman, and seemingly one with a bad reputation. She had three strikes against her in the eyes of many, but not Jesus. That day the Samaritan woman encountered someone who did not ignore her, to whom she was not invisible. He actually spoke to her and continued to do so. He treated her like a human being, with dignity and respect, as if she were valued goods, not damaged ones. No one was ever damaged goods to Jesus.

Once I gave my wife a small potted plant. Even though she's a farmer's daughter, at that time, she really didn't have a green thumb. In fact, it used to be a joke around our house not to give Debbie plants because she would just kill them. Well, she put this plant somewhere in the house and forgot about it for weeks. When we came across it again, the plant looked dead. The leaves were shriveled; the soil was dry as dust. Debbie took it to the kitchen anyway and watered it and continued to water it every couple of days. We thought we'd have to throw the plant away; but one day when I was at the sink, I noticed that the plant had green leaves. It was alive! We thought it damaged and dead beyond repair, but it had been brought back to life with some tender care and water.

The woman at the well was like the plant. She was dry and thirsty, damaged beyond hope of repair, until she met a man with a green thumb, a master gardener. He had just the water and care she needed, and she began to come alive again.

It's true that most people never looked at the cans in the basket we marked as "Damaged Goods. Cheap." But one man, Mr. Christopher, was a regular customer. He would always go to the damaged goods basket and choose several items. When I asked him why he did that when most other people didn't, he replied, "Nothing's really wrong with these," holding up a can that had part of the label gone and several dents. "It's just bent up a little. On the inside it's as good as the ones on the shelves; and it's what's on the inside that counts, isn't it?"

Lord, we are glad your eyes do not just stop on the outside. You see inside, our needs, our thirst, our worth. May we all hear you say, "Come out of that damaged goods basket. That's not for you any-more. You've been bought with a price, a great price." Amen.

The Empty Mailbox

Religion that is pure and undefiled before God, the Father, is this: to care for orphans and widows in their distress (James 1:27).

I was driving into town to visit in the hospital when I saw her. She was creeping her way out to check her mail, wearing a black sweater over a dingy white dress. Stooped over and grasping a cane with a gnarled hand, she reached up and pulled down the lid of the mailbox. Her expression is seared into my mind forever—for the mailbox was empty. I had the strangest feeling that that empty mailbox summed up her whole life as her eyes met mine. No letters. No one, family or friends, caring enough to write to her. Even advertisers had given up on her.

As I drove by, I watched her shut the empty mailbox and look up to heaven as if in a prayerful complaint. Then she began creeping her way back to her empty house.

When I went back that direction later that day, I stopped at the house. From the mailbox I learned that the woman's name was Mrs. Anderson. I knocked on her door, and it took quite awhile before she came to answer. She must have had some hearing impairment, as I had to knock so hard that my knuckles were stinging. I greeted her, told her who I was (but not that I had seen her earlier at the mailbox and felt sorry for her). When she found out I was a minister, her face brightened. I learned she initially thought I was an insurance salesman.

Mrs. Anderson had smudges of something white on her sweater and face. She tried to wipe them off and also to pull strands of her gray hair back into place. She explained that she was making some homemade biscuits and had some fresh jars of apple jelly. She did not have to say anything else. We sat at her tiny kitchen table and had a feast together. It reminded me of the many times I had done the same thing with my grandmother.

I learned much about Mrs. Anderson that day. She had been a widow for thirty-five years. Her two children lived far away. She had seven grandchildren and three great-grandchildren. She collected ceramic cats (loved real cats but it hurt too much when they died, she told me, so she had not had one for a long time). She also made exquisite knitted items that decorated her home.

We became friends that day, and I often stopped by to see Mrs. Anderson. When I could not go by, I always took time to send her a note (so that mailbox would not be empty again).

When we discovered that Mrs. Anderson had nothing planned for Christmas that year, we invited her to our home on Christmas Eve for a special dinner. There was also a large box under the tree for her from our daughter. Mrs. Anderson opened it, and a smile spread over her wrinkled face when she saw looking up at her the face of a snow white kitten. She later named him "Snowball." That smile replaced the frown she had that day beside the empty mailbox.

Sometime later, Mrs. Anderson died in her sleep one night, with Snowball asleep on the pillow beside her. I felt like the empty mailbox when I heard, yet also filled with the special love and the stories she shared with us. Snowball is playing with a ball of string at my feet as I write these words.

Lord, we know there are lots of Mrs. Andersons with mailboxes more empty than full. How easily we drive past them, unaware of their emptiness and of all they have to give. Help us to remember that our faith is indeed shallow if it does not lead us to slow down, see them, and make room for them in our lives. To do so is also to make more room for you. Amen.

"I Didn't Know You, Did I?"

Therefore Saul took a sword, and fell upon it. . . . And David lamented with this lamentation over Saul (1 Samuel 31:4; 2 Samuel 1:17, KJV).

I WILL NEVER FORGET THE DAY WHEN OUR SENIOR minister called the staff together and in a hushed, somber voice told us, "James is dead."

James was my friend. He had served as associate pastor on our church staff. He left our church to assume his first charge as senior minister. One cold afternoon in November of that same year, his fiancée found him in the basement of his parsonage. He had taken his life.

James's death took all of us by surprise. We were stunned. Numbed. Angry. But most of all profoundly sad.

I learned that I never really knew James. Yes, I worked closely with him. We would spend hours talking together. He and his fiancée came over to eat with us on several occasions. But I never really knew him. As I looked back on our conversations, I realized suddenly that they were superficial and shallow. We never really opened up and poured out our souls to one another, took off the masks and revealed who we were.

After the death of James, I wanted to go around to everybody in our church and to my family and friends, grab them by the shoulders, and shake them until they told me everything that had ever bothered them, even if they had to make up something. You see, I learned that I didn't really know them either.

One of the saddest things I have ever heard was said by a young man after the funeral of his father. He said, "I never knew my father. He never really knew me."

Human relationships are not meant to be this way. They do not have to be this way.

One Sunday I began a church school class session by asking the members to share with the whole group something about themselves that few people knew. I expected them to share things that put them in a good light, things that would flatter them. That is about how it went until it was the turn of one young woman. She said, "Well, I guess most people do not know that I am a recovering alcoholic." You could have heard a pin drop.

That woman's honesty made a tremendous

impact on the class over the next few weeks and months, drawing us closer together. We started to truly get to know one another because one person bravely shared who she was, freeing the rest of us to do the same.

The young man said, "I never knew my father. My father never really knew me." It's too late for them now.

I never really knew James. It's too late for that to happen this side of heaven.

But it's not too late for us. There's still time to get to really know one another.

I took my young daughter to the funeral of James so she could say goodbye, for he had been like an uncle to her. In her childlike way she told him that she hoped he would feel better. As we walked out of the service that night, I found myself hoping and praying the same thing.

Loving Lord, you know all we feel, all we think, all we can ever experience. You are always there for us. Help us to cast all our cares upon you, for we know you care for us no matter what. In our brokenness may we truly know the power of your grace. You surround us with persons who long to listen to and care for us. Help us to be willing to share our burdens with them. Help us too to keep on living in faith and love, even in the midst of profound sadness and confusion. Amen.

Time

So teach us to count our days / that we may gain a wise heart (Psalm 90:12).

*D*avid, a friend of mine, took his young son, Justin, to cut some firewood. Noting that he was cutting large pieces, his son said to him, "Daddy, are you going to make some small ones so I can help?" "Yeah, I guess so," he replied. "Because if you aren't," his son continued, "you're wasting my time!"

As I grow older, I sometimes wish I could save time in a bottle, freeze it, or at least slow it down just a little. If only life was like a football game so you could call, "Time out!" and the clock would stop. But time waits for no one, does it?

I really began to realize how time flies after I became a parent. I look around sometimes for that little boy who it seems was bouncing on my knee yesterday but find him only in my memory. In his place is a tall, handsome young man who has just graduated from high school. Instead of the tiny girl whose fingers could not even wrap around one of mine, there stands a lovely young woman who has just begun high school.

I recall when my children first looked at our wedding album. Their remark was, "Dad, you used to be skinny and had hair."

"Yeah, that was BC," I replied.

"What does that mean?" they asked.

"Before Children," I answered; and we all laughed together.

Someone has said that having teenage children is a sign of middle age and also helps bring it on. Well, they certainly give you a very visual reminder every day that time flies. Time is truly an "ever-rolling stream."

I will never forget something that happened to me while walking down the sidewalk in a strange city. I came to the city cemetery and there was something unusual about it. A tall stone column was in the middle with a clock face on each side, so that wherever you stood in that cemetery, you could see the time. Why in the world would anyone put clocks there? The people buried in that place certainly did not need one. As I stood there thinking, the cemetery clock began to chime; and the time of day went echoing throughout the cemetery and out into the city. Suddenly I realized that the clock was not just telling us the time of day but something much more profound:

Time is the stuff life is made of—your life, all lives, the lives of all those who once lived but who lie here now. Time is God's precious gift to you. Do not waste it. Learn to use it wisely.

No one on a deathbed ever said, "I wish I had spent more time at the office." Instead they say, "I wish I had spent more time with God, with my family, with those relationships that now I realize are the most important things of all."

A woman who had just celebrated her one-hundredth birthday was being interviewed for a television show. At one point, her young interviewer asked, "What was life like in your day?" With a polite but cool smile, the elderly lady replied, "THIS is my day!"

This is *your* day! This is *your* time! Use it well. Use it in getting closer to God each day. Use it in those activities that will enrich your life, your mind, your soul. Use it to enrich the lives of all those you touch.

Lord, teach us to number our days, to realize how short our life is, that we may become wise. Amen.

Hold Your Head Up

I lift up my eyes to the hills— / from where will my help come? / My help comes from the LORD, / who made heaven and earth (Psalm 121:1-2).

To you I lift up my eyes, / O you who are enthroned in the heavens! (Psalm 123:1).

W HEN I WAS GROWING UP, I LIVED FOR BASEBALL. I loved it. And, if I say so myself, I was pretty good at playing it. I remember one game right after I got glasses. I was really having problems adjusting to them. I missed two easy fly balls, which left our team behind several runs. I came to the bench with my head bowed. I felt so bad that I didn't want to look at anyone.

Suddenly, I felt a hand on my shoulder; and there was my coach who told me, "Hold your head up!" When I looked up, I saw a coach who still believed in me and friends to encourage me. I wanted to look down, for that's how I felt; but they would not let me.

That's what I find so often in the Bible. "I lift up my eyes to you," the psalmist sings. "Hold your head up! Keep your eyes on God!" is the message.

Lots of experiences will make us want to fasten our eyes on the ground or sink us into depression, so that we withdraw into our own little world. All we can see is our pain, our guilt, our limitations, what we can't do, what we don't have. Looking down all the time makes us down. It limits us. We can see only a few feet. That's the circumference of our world. But it doesn't have to be! Our eyes are to be up, not down. Our vision is set to the horizon. For ours is a faith in a God bigger than our circumstances, a God, the psalmist says, who is "enthroned in the heavens." He forced his eyes toward the heavens to remind himself that the one who made the heavens and the earth certainly had the power to lift him up.

Where we keep our eyes on our journey makes all the difference. Do we keep them on our feet? Are we constantly looking back? Is our mind set just on how very far yet we have to go? Or are our eyes on the horizon? Are we taking each step with expectation of any moment encountering God?

A dear elderly friend of mine has told me more than once, "There is a lot to see if you keep your head up."

I will never forget hearing about a man who was captured during World War II. His captors found out that he was a barber and made him cut hair for all the prisoners. The guards watched and listened closely whenever the barber was working for anything amiss or whispers of an escape attempt. All they heard constantly from the barber as he made sure to have eye contact with each prisoner was, "Keep your head up! Hold your head up!" The guards thought his words were just an instruction. But they were far more. That barber helped save the lives of many in the camp through his constant encouragement: "Keep your head up!"

We all are on a journey. Lots of times the road is rough and steep. We look ahead and wonder how in the world we can keep going. But hold your head up! Look above the road to the One who calls you forward, who is with you each step of the way, and from whom not even death can take you away. Lift up your eyes to the One enthroned in the heavens. And never, ever turn them away. Hold your head up!

God, we journey with our eyes on you. Forgive us when we have taken them away and placed them on other things. Forgive us when we have made the journey of our brothers or sisters harder, rather than lifting them up and encouraging them with our words and actions to hold their head up. Give all our fellow pilgrims on this journey the best gift of all—the constant sense that you are walking each step beside them. Amen.